How to Build a Million-Dollar Business Using the Right Mindset

Sensible Tips on How to Be a Millionaire

By: George Campbell

9781635014969

PUBLISHERS NOTES

Disclaimer – Speedy Publishing LLC

Speedy Publishing LLC

40 E Main Street, Newark, Delaware, 19711

Contact Us: 1-888-248-4521

Website: http://www.speedypublishing.co

REPRINTED Paperback Edition: 9781635014969:

Manufactured in the United States of America

DEDICATION

This book is dedicated to my dad. See you in heaven.

TABLE OF CONTENTS

CHAPTER 1- THE ANATOMY OF ONLINE BUSINESS FAILURE

Every day out there in the real brick and mortar world, millions and millions of people drag themselves from the warm, warm beds, take a shower, grab a cup of coffee, and head off to their jobs as they are thinking that there has got to be an easier way to make a living. Every one of those millions and millions of people knows somebody who has quit the 'get-up-and-go-to-work' grind and is making a very good living by working on their personal computers from the comfort of their own homes.

Working from home sounds like an ideal solution to them. Many of these dissatisfied souls will quit their jobs and plunge head-first into internet marketing with no preparation, no knowledge of what they are doing, no education, and no hope of success. Failure is their only option and they don't even suspect.

The fact is that according to many sources, more than 90% (Ninety percent) of all Internet business start-ups end in failure within the first 120 (one hundred twenty) days. Yes, you read that right. NINETY PERCENT! This failure rate should be a warning to those who are considering trying their hand at making a go of working on the Internet rather than at a job in the brick and mortar world. Of course, success is possible. There IS that other 10% (ten percent) that do succeed.

The thing is success doesn't happen by accident. And success isn't just a crap shoot. Success happens because of some very important factors. Success happens because people have the right ideas about internet marketing and how it works. They do not expect to get rich quick or be able to make a killing overnight and retire to a tropical isle. It is strange but somehow the same people, who wouldn't dream of starting a real world business, think they can make a go of an internet business even though they have no business background. People will go into an internet business with the idea that they no longer have to get up and go to work. They think they can simply work when the feel like it and still make a good living. They simply do not expect to have to work hard or work long hours.

Forget What You Think About the Internet

The 90% failure rate of new Internet businesses really isn't all that surprising when you stop to think about the people who are starting internet businesses. For some unknown reason most people think that running a successful internet business is as easy as getting a website built and hanging out an 'open for business' sign. They couldn't be more wrong. Running a successful internet business of any kind requires self-discipline. People will start an internet business and think that they can party all night, sleep until noon and then make a living in 3 or 4 hours sitting in front of a computer. They somehow think that the world is just going to line up on their website and hand over money. It isn't going to happen. Internet businesses do not run on auto-pilot. It is true that well established internet marketing gurus do not have to put in long, tedious hours on their businesses but it is a privilege that that has been earned by putting in a lot of long and tedious hours. It didn't happen overnight for them and it won't happen overnight for anybody. Most people are totally unprepared for the time investment that must be made in order for an internet business to become successful.

You Have No Idea What You're Doing

All businesses have two things in common. They are BUSINESSES and they must be run like businesses! The people who are in charge of a business need to understand the accepted practices of business. They need to understand simple and basic ideas like acceptable over-head expenses in relation to projected income. Internet entrepreneurs need to understand profit and loss and what constitutes each. A college degree in business in not essential for an internet business entrepreneur go be successful but it sure wouldn't hurt. Just some basic business knowledge is absolutely vital. If you have a hard time balancing your personal check book, you probably should keep your day job and forget about starting an internet business.

It is true that you can hire accounting firms that will tell you WHEN you must make tax deposits, for example, but these firms will not be able to tell you IF you need to make them. Accounting firms can tell you whether or not you made a profit but not how to make it. If you have no business background you need to, at the very minimum, get some good business advice before you even consider opening an online business. The fact is that all successful businesses operate on sound business principles.

Successful businesses aren't accidents. The proof is in the numbers....only 10% of new internet businesses are successful or are even still in existence after the first 120 days of operation. It is not even reasonable to expect to make a profit from a new business enterprise for many, many months. You must have sufficient resources available to not only launch your business but provide for your own personal needs for an extended period of time. It's called 'capital' and there is no way around the need for enough of it.

Meet a Setback, Give Up

You have most likely heard the phrase, 'He has an attitude!" This is usually a derogatory remark made about a person with a disagreeable attitude. But the word 'attitude' is an important one when discussing internet marketing start-ups. A good attitude...a good mind set can't insure success but a bad attitude and a bad mind set can certainly guarantee failure.

Here are some wrong attitudes that will absolutely guarantee failure:

1.I can work when I want to.

Wrong, wrong, wrong! You can't just work when you feel like it. You have to expect to put in many long and very tedious hours of very hard work to make a new internet enterprise succeed.

2.I can get rich quick!

You couldn't be more wrong and you are not only wrong but you are putting yourself in danger as well. There are bazillions of crooks out there on the internet who are waiting for their next easy mark and if you are looking for a quick way to get rich, you ARE the next mark. It is possible to make a very comfortable living with internet marketing enterprises but if anybody ever tells you it is quick or easy, they are lying to you.

3.I don't need a business plan.

There you are...wrong yet again. Internet business is still business. All of the same businesses principles apply to online business as apply to brick and mortar business. It is imperative that you have a plan for success that is based upon these sound business principles.

4.When you have an internet business of your own, you don't have a boss.

Wrong again! You are your boss. If you aren't a good boss who sees to it that works is accomplished on time and in full, you will doom yourself to certain failure. Unless you are a boss who sets up a working schedule and establishes goals that must be met, you will find yourself working at a job under a boss who does do those things and maybe for minimum wage.

How to NOT Fail

The thing about starting a business...any business.....is that there is no guarantee of success under any circumstances. Even big international businesses can fail at new business ventures. Failure is always an option but the possibility of success can be optimized. You can optimize the possibility of success by:

How to Build a Million-Dollar Business Using the Right Mindset

1. Having a good solid business plan in place BEFORE you launch your online business.

There is an old saying: "Those who fail to plan, plan to fail". A detailed set of plans for success needs to be made. You need to have the steps from getting from point A to point B listed in great detail that include realistic cost estimates for accomplishing each step.

2. Expecting to work very hard to accomplish your goals.

You must never expect anything to be easy. You will be right most of the time because things are rarely as easy as they look. Each step toward success requires work, time and patience. Sometimes things don't work out right on the first try. You have to be willing to try again and again until you do succeed.

3. Not falling for 'get-rich-quick schemes.

The internet woods are full of those who prey upon those who are looking for quick and easy ways to become rich. Those ways do not exist. Get over thinking that there is an easy way. There is NOT. Remember those statistics! Ninety percent of all new internet businesses fail in the first 120 days. You don't have to be part of that majority. You can become a part of that 10% minority of successful internet business enterprises.

CHAPTER 2- WHAT MAKES AN ONLINE BUSINESS VENTURE SUCCESSFUL?

Running a successful internet business can look so simple when you are on the outside looking in. You look at a successful internet entrepreneur and he doesn't look like he is doing anything special but he is living the good life. It really doesn't look like he is working all that hard. He seems to be enjoying life immensely. Really...all he is doing is sitting comfortably in front of his own computer in his own very comfortable home a few hours a day. He talks on the telephone and seems to be enjoying every conversation.

Apparently, running a successful internet business is the proverbial 'piece of cake'! Right? WRONG!!! Wrong, wrong, wrong! You are looking at the results of a very, very long and tedious process that consisted of many very long, late-night hours and a lot of blood, sweat and tears over a period of several years. This successful internet entrepreneur worked very, very hard for the success that you are looking at. It is more than a little bit likely that he first placed four corner stones first as he began the long process of building his successful Internet business. Those four corner stones upon which he built his success are:

1. The right mind set.

2. Recognizing and using leverage.

3. Building a set of useful contacts.

4. And he probably had a mentor.

All of them are important, even crucial to the success of any business but especially to the success of an internet based business. Constructing a successful business in cyber space has many things in common with the building of a successful brick and mortar business but there are significant differences as well.

How to Have the Right Mindset

The success of any business both of the online variety as well as the off line variety require the right mindset from the get-go. A right and healthy mind set will not guarantee success but a wrong and unhealthy or unrealistic mindset will most assuredly guarantee failure. So the right mind set is the first corner stone that must be laid upon which a successful business can be constructed. What is a right and healthy mindset? There are things that it is as well as things that it isn't.

A right and healthy mindset IS the willingness to work as hard and as long as is necessary to achieve the goals that has been set. A right and healthy mindset ISN'T the belief that success will be easy, quick or painless. Those who believe that they can make an internet business enterprise thrive without having to actually put in any time or effort are simply doomed to failure from the beginning. There are schemers and scammers out there in cyberspace that are just waiting eagerly for those to come along who are looking for easy riches. A right and healthy mindset IS the willingness to take the time to make a good, solid business plan that is based upon sound business principles. A right and healthy mindset ISN'T just jumping in feet first and hoping for the best.

The best that can happen under those circumstances is that you get out with any more than two cents to your name. 'Flying by the seat of your pants' is NOT a plan...it is just plain suicide in the world of internet marketing. If you don't have a formal education in business, you need to find people who do have that kind of education and seek then follow their advice. Choosing the Right Business Model to Use There are dozens...maybe hundreds....of business models out there. Some are, of course, more successful than others but they all come with their own set of pros and cons. The idea is to get the most bang for the buck. You need to use all of the power of the Internet to make your e-business successful.

You really cannot afford to leave any stone unturned. If you are a real go-getter, the temptation is to do everything first and that isn't possible. You need to make a realistic plan and build one thing upon another until you have a good solid base from which to operate. Once you get a website built, you will need to begin leveraging SEO (search engine optimization) and gaining page rank. One thing does lead to another, of course, but one of the quickest ways to leverage SEO is to add a blog to your website. This is a way that you can get much more quickly indexed by the search engines.

Leveraging also includes branding yourself, your website and your products. One of the quicker ways to begin to get you branded is by investing in PLR (Private Label Rights) products and changing the names of those products to include your own name or logo. (Don't forget that there must be some rewriting done.) This is probably the quickest way to become branded as well as gain credibility on the internet.

For example: you might by a PLR E-Book about Easy Dog Training and change the name to 'John Doe's Easy Dog Training Methods'. You can sell the book, give it away as a free gift on your own website or list it in E-Book repositories for others to use. Remember that reputation and credibility are everything on the internet. Don't take any shortcuts and never damage or allow others to damage either.

Who Do You Know In Your Niche?

That is an old saying. "It is not What you know, but Who you know that counts". Setting a corner stone of good solid relationships is an important aspect of building a successful e-enterprise. Working hard at building good solid business relationships is worth every minute of time that you invest in it.

Business relationship building should be one of your top priorities. When you build social relationships, you insert yourself into social situations where you come in contact with people who have interests that are similar to or complimentary to your own interests don't you? That is precisely the same way that business relationships are established. You insert yourself into business situations where you will meet others who have businesses that are similar to or complimentary to your own business. You develop relationships over a period of time.

There are several ways in which to accomplish this task. One way is to participate in teleseminars or webinars that are related to your business. You will learn a lot, of course, but equally important, you will come in contact with those who are already succeeding in the niche market that you are working in. Of course, attending real brick and mortar world seminars is an even better way to begin to build friendly business relationships with not only your peers but also with those who are in a position to help you....which brings me to the final corner stone that you need to lay.

Trust in the Expertise of Mentors

It isn't likely that there is a more valuable asset that a new e-entrepreneur can have than a good and capable mentor. Someone who has already made all of the mistakes can help you to avoid making all of the mistakes yourself. They have the wisdom that comes from experience to point out pitfalls and to help direct you toward the better of choices. Why, you ask, would anyone who has it made want to take their time to help a newbie succeed? Maybe I can answer that by telling you about my friend who is an accomplished musician. He played with some of the biggest stars in the business. He is a very, very fine guitarist who is now in his 70's. He has about three young guitarists that he spends many hours not only teaching how to play but counseling them on career choices. I asked him why he spent so much time doing that and he said, "It is like gaining immortality. If I teach them and they teach others, then what I know lives forever."

Successful internet marketers want that 'immortality' as well. The ones who are the very most successful are the ones, amazingly enough, who are the most likely to mentor an up and coming e-entrepreneur. Of course, these successful internet marketers are not going to be interested in wasting their time on a person who has not already worked hard to lay those first three corner stones themselves.

These potential mentors are looking for new comers who show that they have a right and healthy mindset, who are working hard at leveraging and who are well aware of how important it is to know all the players and the RIGHT people. It short, the new comer most likely to get a mentor is one who is already working hard and helping himself and not looking for someone who can just smooth the way for him.

Chapter 3- How to Keep Your Online Business above Your Competitors

Grow or die! This is one of the laws of nature that applies to all living things. All business lives by this law as well. A business cannot begin, grow to a certain point and then simply remain at that point and continue to thrive. Growth and expansion are necessary for the business to survive and if that growth and expansion do not happen then the business will fade and die or crash and burn.

Growth and expansion of business must be controlled by the business owners or managers. If growth is too slow, the business lags behind the competition. If growth is too fast, the business can easily become over extended. A steady controlled growth is the ideal. Of course, the ideal and the reality are sometimes two very different things. Sometimes the terms 'growth and expansion' are a bit misunderstood. The most obvious meaning of both terms is to get bigger and broader but those meanings are not the only ones that apply. Growth, for example, can mean gaining knowledge and becoming wiser and expansion can mean broadening the knowledge base from which a company operates.

A small internet based company does not have to grow and expand until it becomes a giant multi-national company in order to survive but the owners and managers of these internet businesses do have to grow by getting smarter and expand by welcoming change with open arms. Nothing ever just stays the same. Change is the only certainty in the world. What was hot or what worked yesterday is old news today and it will be ancient history tomorrow. Companies and company owners and managers must grow with and adapt to changes as they happen and on the internet changes happen a lot faster than they do out in the brick and mortar world. We all agree that growing, adapting and expanding is vital to the survival of any business and maybe especially to Internet business.

So the question is: What is the key to growth and expansion of internet based businesses? When brick and mortar businesses grow and expand, they build bigger buildings and hire more employees but that isn't exactly an option for an internet based business. The key to growth and expansion of an internet based business is for the business owner or manager to always and continuously invest in them. They must be willing to stay on the cutting edge of technology and they must be willing to accept and adapt to changes as they occur. Internet businesses are not buildings. Internet businesses are people.

An internet business cannot grow by investing in a larger building. It only grows when the person who is driving that business invests in his or her own knowledge and ability. An internet business cannot expand by investing in hiring more people. An internet business expands when the person who is driving it invests in himself or herself. The bottom line is this: The key to continuous growth and expansion of an internet based business is continuous investments being made in the owner or manager of the business. The short answer: Invest in yourself.

Why Should You Invest in Yourself?

You have no doubt heard this refrain many times. "Invest in yourself! Invest in yourself! Invest is yourself!" But what does 'invest in yourself' mean? Does it mean you should go out and invest in a haircut that costs two hundred bucks? Does it mean that you should go by yourself a designer suit? What does it mean to invest in yourself? Well, if you can afford it, go get that haircut and buy that designer suit but that is not the kind of investment that we are talking about here. Your internet business is just you, your computer and your internet connection and you could actually operate your internet business from any commuter on the planet that had an internet connection. So basically, your business is really only you. Your business is based only upon your own knowledge and your own ability. Those are the 'company' assets and those are the ones that need to grow and expand constantly so that your internet business thrives.

Here is a rule that you might want to live by to insure that your internet business is a success and continues to be a success: Invest 5% of your time and income into improving yourself. Expansion and growth are imperative to survival and expansion and growth of an internet business means expanding and growing the knowledge of the person running the company...that would be YOU.

A tiny investment of only 5% of your time and your income per year in yourself can mean that you will continue to see positive monetary returns for many, many years to come. You might be sitting there shaking your head and still wondering what is meant by a 5% time and income investment per year in yourself. What is meant is that you must expand your knowledge. You must stay on top of new technological advancements and you must expand your knowledge base about your own area of expertise. Things change fast. New information becomes available on almost everything under the sun every day of the week. It is very, very easy to fall behind very, very quickly. And unless you consciously put forth the effort to stay on top of things you will most certainly fall behind.

Keeping up is easier than catching up and if you keep up, you can usually find a way to forge ahead. Yes, you are so busy right now that you could use 48 hour days but taking just about one hour per day out of the 24 that you are allotted and only $5 out of every hundred dollars that you earn and investing that time and money in yourself can increase your future earnings a hundred fold. There are newsletters, webinars, teleseminars and real brick and mortar seminars that can provide information and cause your knowledge to grow and expand so that your business can also grow and expand but you must be willing to invest in yourself so that you can take advantage of this information...learn it...and apply it to your own internet business.

Top Self-Investment Tips that Work Wonders

It is absolutely true that time is the one commodity that most internet entrepreneurs have a very, very short supply of. Still there are ways to use time that would otherwise be of no value to invest in yourself. Here are a few tips that might help:

• Use travel time to invest in yourself. By using your iPod or your MP3 player you can use your travel time to expand your knowledge.

- Set your clock for a half hour earlier and use that time to read and learn.

- After you stop working in the evening, use your computer to search for new information and ideas. Of course there are some things that are just going to take your time but you can choose wisely.

- Attend webinars and teleseminars that are directly related to your niche or your business.

- Attend real world seminars that are closer to your home and will require less travel time but will provide you with the information that you need.

Step Out Of Your Comfort Zone

We all have a comfort zone and all of us are very fond of our personal comfort zone. It is very, very tempting to just stick with doing the things that we have always done and doing them in the same way we have always done them. However, staying in your comfort zone and refusing to expand your mind and your horizons can cause you and your internet business to fail. There is an old saying (probably made up by someone who was afraid of trying new things) that says, "If it isn't broke, don't fix it." Well, 'it' doesn't have to be broken in order to be improved upon whatever 'it' is. Candle light wasn't broken but we are all glad that electricity was harnessed. Electric light is still light but it is certainly a big improvement over candle light.

New ideas come along every day in the world of internet business. Some of those ideas are even good ones even if they do reside outside of our own personal comfort zone. In order to continue to invest in yourself, you must be willing to leave your own comfort zone. Just because what has worked is still working it doesn't mean that there are not newer, better and more efficient ways of doing things. Nobody is saying that new is always better. New is not always better but sometimes it is and the only way to tell which is which is by investigating new ideas yourself and then adapting the ones that can help you to your business.

Invest in yourself by increasing your knowledge and don't be afraid of trying new things and new ways of doing things. These things really are the secrets of success and not just in the world of internet business but in life itself.

CHAPTER 4- ARE YOU BUILT FOR AN ENTREPRENEURIAL LIFE?

A person who is constantly in pursuit of new ventures, the one who is high on risk taking especially when it comes to financial risk is an entrepreneur. This very word can be applied to a person who is initiating an opportunity or a new project; however it is mostly used in the context of a person who is in pursuit of new ventures in the field of business. The basic traits of such an individual are often characterized as a person who is optimistic, hard-working, risk-taker, innovative, independent and creative.

Sometimes entrepreneurs are also called the 'creative destruction'; this is because they are constantly on the lookout for redesigning and renovating the traditional and standard services and products in order to bring out a new innovative dimension that could possibly give a boost to the organizations. They constantly try to reinvigorate the already existing market by introducing new methodologies, be it in production, structure or in organization. Because of their high risk-taking ability they may even tear down the already existing companies. The way they do the business is by the means of entirely developing the products or the services that may cause an older variation to become irrelevant or even obsolete sometimes. One of the examples of this is the advancements in automobiles which has caused the horse drawn carriage industry to become obsolete.

RISK FACTOR

'Risk-taking' is a basic characteristic trait of an entrepreneur. But this doesn't mean that there is complete tolerance for risk in an entrepreneur, as a matter of consideration a successful entrepreneur knows how to determine how much risk must be taken for a specific endeavor. In order to introduce something new to the market one has to take enough risk, which gives a scope to innovation and creativity, so much so that the business or the activity is profitable.

The most basic thing that the entrepreneur risks in market is his money. Often times they put in the money they have as well as of the parties into the projects, the failure of which can not only cause a loss to the financers but also to the savings and livelihood of the entrepreneurs themselves. And if the project succeeds they enjoy great financial rewards as well. There are various other kinds of risks that are also involved in the lives of entrepreneurs. The entrepreneurs may also face social risk factors in case the societal norms are challenged by their innovations, or any kind of psychological risk due to the hard work they do. It is often felt that the feeling of notoriety, sense of contribution to the betterment of the society and the independence often outweighs the dangers of the risks involved with the lives of an entrepreneur, although it seldom happens that the rewards are apparent immediately.

Characteristics and Traits:

Some of the additional traits of the entrepreneurs comprise of spontaneity as well as unique creativity; a willingness to form decisions with or without a solid data in hand. The drive to create something new or tangible is often the purpose of the whole existence of entrepreneurs. There dare-devil ability to thrive on the risk factor and involvement with new enterprises that have low rate of success requires a great deal of ability, patience and perseverance. These entrepreneurs have a great hand at success as they bring out the new and unconventional ideas that might click in the market and become a great success.

The societal value of the entrepreneurs and their spirit is very high. In order to encourage them and their activities, major governmental as well as non-governmental organizations sponsor them arranging access to tax exemption, advice on management and inexpensive capital. As a matter of fact, various universities have established 'business incubators' especially for entrepreneurs in hope of turning their research into products that can be marketed as innovations. These innovations and the technologies that come as a result of these innovations may lead to the industrial development that may further give boost to the society as more revenues and jobs would be provided to the people.

However, being an entrepreneur is not the same thing as running a business, even though there are many things that overlap the two areas. Entrepreneurs are mostly independent people, so if their ventures succeed this independency may cause a few problems. Usually they are very much capable of taking care of and managing a small company with almost all the aspects of the business, but after a considerable amount of growth in the company it becomes a little difficult for the entrepreneur to manage it alone. There may be a conflict in the management if the entrepreneur fails to recognize that managing a growing company is very much different from managing a small and stable company. Often the entrepreneur is seeking new innovations as well as taking risks and chances which might not be a very suitable idea for the manager of a stable company, who on the other hand might be focused on establishing a brand and building sales. Such issues can be resolved if the entrepreneur takes up a new venture leaving the company behind, adapting and adjusting to the new priorities set, or being forced to quit.

Another readily noticeable characteristic of an entrepreneur is his self-confidence. This is a very important aspect since entrepreneurs attempt to succeed commonly with the help of new ideas. It is generally seen that often time people are skeptical of the ideas of entrepreneurs that have not been proven that they could be of any use, or sometimes when the aspirant entrepreneur attempts to achieve great heights and people do not perceive him to do so good. This is the very reason that entrepreneurs get a lot of support from the inner resources.

Entrepreneurs are the people who have the tendency to be highly driven and unlike many others who are comfortable working as employees, they do not require the threat of the hierarchy to act upon what is to be done for the company. Most of the entrepreneurs do not depend upon other people for encouragement for acting on their ideas or for any other motivation. The one who is an entrepreneur constantly works towards their goals with an urgency that is generated by them. The list of tasks that are to be completed by the entrepreneur is a long one in order for him to realize his goal. The one who is able to delegate most of these responsibilities to others in order to achieve his task is the fortunate one; however many times an entrepreneur has to rely on himself till he achieves success to a certain degree. Keeping such situations in mind the characteristics of an entrepreneur must include being a persistent hard-worker and ability to multi-task.

Perseverance is also a key factor of their characteristics. It is almost impossible to find an entrepreneur who has achieved his goals very easily with no obstacles. There are often times when they have to face the gravest of failures. But it is the strength of their character that makes them so strong and they refuse to give up and succumb to failures, moreover changing the failures into a new challenge. Finally entrepreneurs have the ability for great detail, since it is necessary to focus on the minute details in order to achieve a goal with precision. For instance, the entrepreneurs have to deal with the costs at one point or another in their ventures by streamlining it. Also a great deal of concentration is put into the technical aspects in order to locate the tiny glitch that is creating a major problem in production. A big part is being able to tackle these hurdles.

What are the Skills You Need?

The basic skills that are required for a successful entrepreneur to have are having good money and time management skills. The aspirant must be able to concentrate as well as must engage in multiple tasks all at once without being heedless to any one task at hand. The skill that marks a successful entrepreneur is the ability to possess fearlessness in order to act on new opportunities and the tact to recognize them as well.

How to Build a Million-Dollar Business Using the Right Mindset

It is required for an entrepreneur to have excellent communication skills, the job of an entrepreneur requires him/her to be constantly putting forth their ideas, efforts and talents to different kinds of people in the organization and he/she must be able to communicate well with them all. If the communication is not good, there might be difficulties in getting support or recognition or to build clientele. Apart from the communication an entrepreneur must be able to listen to the advises and opinions from others even if he doesn't want to, apart from that to maintain the flow of communication and to be well informed about the company and the ventures.

Managing time is an essential skill that the entrepreneur must possess. The people who are the employees have a given objective and a given time in which they have to complete a given task, however in the case of an entrepreneur, the guidelines and goals are set by himself in order for him to achieve them and a successful entrepreneur knows how to manage his time well in order to realize his goals as fast as he can.

Money management is also a very crucial skill that an entrepreneur must possess. In case the entrepreneur is highly skilled at making money but tends to become careless afterwards, there are chances that he might experience failure due to it. An efficient entrepreneur knows how to invest his money and also save a lot wisely so as not to cause havoc when the venture or ideas fail which may cause a loss of money. So a successful entrepreneur must be able to spend as well as save his money wisely in order to direct efficiently towards his goals.

Although most people do not see it as a skill, it is very important that an entrepreneur is able to concentrate well on minute details of different tasks in a venture in order to achieve his/her goal. If the mind is scattered and an entrepreneur is unable to constantly focus on his tasks, the chances are that he might face a lot of difficulty in realizing his goals in the ventures at hand, as they may find that are chasing multiple ideas to no avail. Apart from concentration, another essential skill for becoming a successful entrepreneur is the ability to multi-task on various tasks all at once. Multi-tasking is the skill which should be at the top of the list of abilities that an entrepreneur must possess, as an entrepreneur seldom has the luxury of taking up and finishing one task at one time. On the contrary, it is required for an entrepreneur to be engaged actively in multiple things at once on which he/she must devote equal attention as well as effort.

Finally the list of the skills required to become a successful entrepreneur is incomplete without the ability to recognize the opportunities. If an entrepreneur is too focused on a single thing and in one single direction, the growth in the operation gets stifled and it takes a lot of effort to manage the business ideas and the person has to struggle through it. So it is very important that the entrepreneur recognizes the opportunity when he/she sees it, in order to analyze it carefully and to act on it.

CHAPTER 5- WORK VS. DEALS

Just about every internet marketer that I have ever known has worked at some kind of job other than internet marketing before they launched their internet marketing careers. It is a funny thing about working at a job that pays you for the work that you do. You get into a 'work-equals- money' mindset. After all, when you work for others, work does, in fact, equal money. But when you launch an internet marketing career the 'work' that used to make money for you now prevents you from making money. It is true.

The 'work' that you are doing that you once got paid to do, like answering the telephone, answering emails, filing papers, etc. is actually preventing you from making the deals that will put money in your pocket. Yet we continue to seek work because we are programmed to think of work as the thing that makes money. We get stuck in the 'work-equals-money' mindset that is actually

George Campbell

counterproductive to building a successful internet marketing business.

We focus our time and energy on finding work for ourselves rather than on focusing our time and energy on making the deals that will really make money for us. It isn't hard to see why we get into this 'work-equals-money' mindset. We have been living with that concept since we were kids. Think about it.

What was your first job? Did you cut grass for a neighbor? Didn't you get money after you had done the work? Of course, you did. He wasn't paying you to think...he was paying you to cut grass. When you got older and got a job at the local burger joint, you got paid for cooking hamburgers and French Fries. You cooked the hamburgers and fries and then you got paid. Word did in fact equal money. The owner of the hamburger joint wasn't paying you to find a better way to cook hamburgers or paying you to look for a new market to sell hamburgers. He was only paying you for doing the work of cooking the hamburgers. But now you are not getting paid for doing the 'work'.

The work isn't what is making money for you. It is true that the work must still be done but you don't have to look for it. It will find you. What you need to be looking for now are the deals that will make you money.

What is Work Made Up Of?

What is 'work'? The 'work' that makes any business work is just the day to day activities that must be accomplished in order for the business to function. Telephone calls must be answered. Emails must be read and responded to. Files must be kept orderly. The list goes on and on but this is just 'work'. Nobody is going to pay you to answer the phone, read emails or keep files in order. That is simply 'work' that must be done. It isn't making you any money and it most certainly is not what you should be focused upon.

Once an internet marketing business has gotten up and running, it is a very good investment to simply pay a virtual assistant to do the 'work' and set yourself free to make the deals that actually make you money and make your internet marketing business thrive. You can't do this right away, of course, but you can use as little of your time as possible on mundane tasks. You can spend hours and hours and hours of your time working on your website....making it better...tweaking this and tweaking that. That is work that is not putting a single red cent into your bank account.

Hire a techie to do that 'work' for you while you are making deals that make more than enough to pay the techie. Until you can hire someone to do this work for you, get it fixed as best you can and move on the productive deal making. How many hours in a day do you spend writing and making posts to your blogs? Is this time actually making any money for you? No, of course, it isn't. It is just 'work'. It is work that others could do just as well or work that you can find ways to make shorter like by using PLR materials rather than writing every word yourself.

Customer service is absolutely vital work that must be done. It must be done quickly and efficiently and above all competently. It might even be work that in the beginning at least that you must do yourself. There are however companies and individuals out there in cyber space that are perfectly capable of handling this work for you and you don't have to make it harder than it needs to be.

George Campbell
What Does Making Deals Mean?

Yes, it is absolutely true that the 'work' must be done, but the work that must be done should be done as quickly and as efficiently as possible and you shouldn't concentrate your energy on finding and creating more work that isn't going to making any money for you. You need to be focusing your attention on making the deals that will make money. Just as soon as you possibly can, you should begin to hire people to do the mundane tasks that must be accomplished and free up as much of your own time as possible for deal making. So what exactly are the activities that constitute deal making?

Briefly and concisely they are the activities that have the potential for putting money into your bank account. A few of these activities are:

1. Visiting forums and blogs that relate to your niche:

Forums and blogs are where you find the real living, breathing people who are YOUR potential customers and until somebody drags out their credit card, puts in their information and actually buys products or services from you, you haven't made a dime so you need to go where the people are and find out how to best serve their wants and needs.

2. Visit websites that are related to your website.

This is where you will find your potential joint venture partners. Contact the webmasters and work on making mutually profitable deals.

3. Start your own newsletter or E-zine:

This is one of the most potentially profitable deals that you can make for yourself. The longer your list grows, the more profits you can make.

4. Attend seminars in the brick and mortar world and build good solid business relationships with others in your field.

Here again are potential joint ventures partners that you need to take the time to cultivate.

5. Put together your own webinar or teleseminar:

Find interesting speakers who would supply information of interest to your list. Webinars and teleseminars are both easy and inexpensive to do. They are also money making deals that you can make.

Should You Quit Work and Focus Only on Deals?

It would really be nice if we could just ditch the work-a-day-work and do nothing with our time other than make the deals that make us money! Now that would be what I would call a perfect world. Unfortunately, the work-a-day-work must be done and until our 'ship comes in' we are probably going to be the ones who have to do that as well as make the deals that make us money.

As long as we are going to have to do both we can at least learn how to work smarter. We can learn how to get the same amount of 'work' accomplished in less time so that we can free up more time for making the deals that will make us money. Some examples of working smarter are:

George Campbell

1. Write a FAQ page for your website and use your autoresponder to direct most questions to that site.

2. Subscribe to a Private Label Rights (PLR) membership website and use that material (with only a little rewrite) as your blog posts and your website content. You can even make whole new products that can be sold from this PLR material.

3. Make a schedule for yourself that allows only so much time for the tasks that must be completed that make you no money and allow more time in that schedule for the deal making tasks that will make you money.

4. Invest in automation software that is designed to take care of simple every day but time consuming tasks.

There is always the 'work' that must be done each and every day but don't let it become the object of your focus. Don't look for work to be done. Work no longer equals money for you now that you are an internet marketer. Get the work done as quickly as you can and put your focus on the deal making activities that will add to your bottom line. It is no longer your job just to make hamburgers...now you need to get out there and look for new markets. You ARE getting paid to think now.

CHAPTER 6- YOUR SUCCESS AND FAILURE IS YOURS TO MAKE

The success (or failure) of your Internet Entrepreneurship really is up to you now. If you succeed, the credit will all belong to you and if you fail, you will own that as well. Your success or failure is in your own hands. Success and failure are two sides of the same coin. The coin in question is your own Internet Entrepreneurship and you don't want to flip that coin into the air and leave it to chance as to whether it lands on success or failure.

You want complete control over the fate of your Internet business and you do have that control. Every decision will be yours to make. If you make wise choices then you will claim victory and success will be yours. If you make unwise choices then your internet business will crash and burn and your own hopes and dreams will go up in flames along with it.

Not Everything Will Be in Your Favor

You do realize, of course, that the odds for success are not in your favor. Every day thousands and thousands of internet business enterprises are launched. Of those internet businesses that will be launched today, 90% (ninety percent) will not be around in 120 days. That is right!

You have no better than a 10% chance of actually making a success out of your internet business unless you can change them those are not very good odds. If it were a horse race, winning would be considered a long shot. That is the down side but anytime there is a down side there is always an upside. The upside in this case is that even though you have only a 10% chance at succeeding, you can greatly better your odds by simply following the guidelines that have already been offered.

You can increase your odds from 10% to 90% by simply applying a few very simple principles to the problem. The reasons that so many new Internet entrepreneurs fail within the first 120 days can be narrowed down to four.

1. They do not have the right mindset.

2. They do not lay a solid foundation.

3. They do not have the key to unlock growth and expansion.

4. They do not plan for success

How to Build a Million-Dollar Business Using the Right Mindset

Think of Success, Believe in It, Work on It

Unfortunately, so many people think that they can quit their jobs, open an internet business and just relax and enjoy life. They expect instant success and instant wealth without having to invest anything (even time and effort) to affect that success. They really believe that they can sleep until noon, work when and if they want to and just rack up sales and profit. This attitude probably accounts for at least half of all of the failures of new internet businesses.

Making an internet business successful takes a lot of time and even more work. That old real world job demanded that you be on the job for probably 40 hours each week. Your net internet business will need about twice that many hours each week if it is to become successful. Very, very, very few people are willing to invest that much time and effort thus the 90% failure rate. Of the few that are willing to put in enough time and effort most expect instant success. They don't even consider the fact that they will need to continue to meet their own personal expenses for many months before they see the first penny of profit from a new internet business even though those facts are readily available.

These are the ones who go out there looking for get-rich-quick schemes and end up becoming victims of internet scam artists. The right mindset is this: You must expect to work hard. You must expect to work long and tedious hours. You will not be an over-night success. People are not going to line up to give you their money. You are going to have to earn it.

Cement the Right Foundation

Sometimes people will start an internet business that has no business background at all. This is another reason for the high failure rate of new internet entrepreneurships. If you do not have an education in business, then you would be very wise indeed to speak with those who are well versed in business. An internet business of any kind is a BUSINESS. It must be run like a business and it must be built upon sound business practices. The only 'dumb' questions are those that are never asked.

You need information and the best way there is to get the information that you need is to simply ask questions of those who have the answers. There are courses available both out in the brick and mortar world as well as on the internet about how to set up and run a successful business. You can't abide by the rules if you don't know what the rules are. Do your homework before you launch your business. You need to lay a rock solid foundation so that your new business doesn't become one of the casualties that are caused by poor planning or even no planning. You need a business plan. You need a business model and it needs to be one that you can understand and follow. Jumping in and hoping for the best isn't a plan. That will only insure that your new internet business will not still be in existence four months from now.

Grow With the Changes of Times

Nothing in this world ever stays the same. The only absolute certainty is change. Internet business is not an exception to this rule. As a matter of fact, business on the internet changes faster than just about anything you can imagine. Another reason that so many new internet businesses don't survive for very long is that a new e-entrepreneur will start a business based upon one single idea and never grow or expand beyond that single idea. These people have what I sometimes call 'tunnel vision'. They don't look around at the internet business landscape and make the necessary changes that keep them visible and a player in the market place.

Internet businesses themselves will naturally grow and expand if the owner or manager of the business grows and expands his knowledge and is willing to adapt to the inevitable changes that take place on a daily basis in Internet business. It is simply good business to invest a minimum of 5% of your time and your income back into yourself. You ARE your business. I've heard the term 'continuing education' tossed about like it was a choice to be made. Continuing education is not a choice if a business is to be successful.

The 10% of new internet businesses that will still be around after the next 120 days will be owned or managed by people who are constantly learning new things and applying those new things to the internet businesses that they operate. They attend real world seminars. They attend teleseminars and webinars. They read multiple newsletters every single day. They learn...they grow....they adapt....they succeed. That is very easy to say but it is much harder to accomplish. However, those who do accomplish it will still be in business when most others are not.

Plan for Success

There is an old saying that I quote very often. "Those who fail to plan, plan to fail!" I say it often because it is the single most important fact of success in a nutshell. A plan for an internet business is just exactly like a road map that would be used for making a road trip. It is a detailed plan of how to get from point A (starting an internet business) to point B (having a successful internet business) in the shortest possible time and without taking the scenic route.

Most of the time, those who begin new internet businesses have been working at jobs where they receive regular paycheck. They are in the 'work equals money' mindset and they bring that mindset into their internet businesses. They will even spend their time searching for more 'work' to do rather than searching for ways in which to make money. Unless the 'work = money' mindset can be quickly changed to 'sales = money' mindset, the business will certainly fail and fail very quickly.

One of the most important items that can be listed in a business plan is to 'find a mentor'. You can have all of the details written down of exactly how you plan to succeed but if you can find a mentor that process can be cut in half. Of course, it is very unlikely that you will find a mentor within the first 120 days of starting your new internet business but that item needs to always be in your mind as you make contacts and build business relationships. Building and internet business is a very exciting undertaking but it is one that is fraught with obstacles. You can overcome the obstacles and succeed but don't expect it to be easy or quick. It will be neither.

CHAPTER 7- BRANCH OFF TO A NEW BUSINESS VENTURE

Among the various types of ideas of getting an entrepreneur breakthrough are the ideas of small business as well as innovative ideas. The ideas of young entrepreneurs may also be discussed in this section. The idea of entrepreneurs may be towards gearing up the starting of a business venture or may be for the expansion of the already existing business. It may also be that they may purchase the shares of a large business and become a franchisee.

The idea of initiating a new business is most common among entrepreneurs. Either one or a group of people may get the idea and concept of a brand new business, or may come to a decision of entering an already popular business. For example, an entrepreneur may either introduce a new product or technology to the market, or may opt to enter with products and technologies already existing in the market, but with a different approach that is unique and creating a new brand name with the products that are familiar and that are differentiated from the rest of such products in the market. So whether or not the business ideas are new or old, the scope of adding a twist to the already existing business or introducing a completely new idea gives the entrepreneurs a limitless scope for improvisation and success.

To initiate a new kind of business requires new innovations and technological inventions. It can be anything from a new concoction to a new technology that the market hasn't witnessed before or a series of new creations. The function of the society can be changed by the unique entrepreneur ideas and introduction of new and unique technologies in to the market. Some of the major evidences that we can see today are the inventions like vaccines, computers, mobile phones, refrigerators, etc.

It is very usual that young and enthusiastic entrepreneurs with fresh ideas grab more and more attention since they are originated from the sources that are unexpected. It is these ideas that have the tendency to create a business and ideas can come from any source, not just highly qualified entrepreneurs but also from young children or young adults, since 'Necessity is the mother of all inventions' and so the young generations are more in need of solutions to their little big issues pertaining to their education or hobby etc. It is mostly seen that children and people in their adolescence are highly imaginative and can think of amazing business ideas. So it is very likely that such gifted youths move ahead to become successful entrepreneurs given that they adapt the characteristics and skills required for this field. The entrepreneurs are usually surrounded by media for their new ideas and also because it has come from a person who is so young.

The ideas of entrepreneurship may also include investment in the brand that is already familiar, for example a franchise of fast food chains or convenience store. Although these are not new or fresh ideas in which an entrepreneur is investing in, but some unique or different idea might be introduced by them in order to make their venture more attractive, user-friendly and different from the others in the market. The entrepreneur may usually purchase a franchise for its strong brand name; hence the entrepreneur has to learn how the franchisor practices the business in order to operate it and to make it grow.

Entrepreneurs are also required to have a deep knowledge about the market and the industry competition in order to make sure whether or not a given idea or new venture would be a success in the market or not. There are five major forces that drive competition in industry.

• The rivalry between the existing firms in market

• The entry of a new and potential competitor in the market

• The development of the substitute products

• The power of bargaining of the suppliers

• And the power of bargaining of the costumers.

However, in modern times the strategies are placed on dynamism, hard completion and fast reaction to new technologies. Although the managers from the past few decades had to face the brutality of competition of the free market, today, information, technology, and globalization are responsible for the growth and significant changes in the revenue. The shifting of patterns of communication and the developments are forcing the companies to deal with issues on an operating level. So eventually, as the boundaries of the competition becomes weak, the rivalries of the constant competitive forces get intensified as well as short, the company then seeks to dynamically develop with some fast changing strategies. In the light of such a competitive atmosphere, the leadership and mindset of an entrepreneur are the foundation on which the new opportunity for the company can be framed. The entrepreneurial strategies also include the growth of a company through market-busting tactics which are basically the moves that are identified and the opportunities are tracked down for the constant strategic growth. Two of the most recent changes that had occurred in the field of entrepreneurship are, that information technology and Internet are playing a major role in creation of new opportunities in the market and that the manager's job, as in the person who attempts to adapt the entrepreneurial mindset has grew tough. After the year 2000, the companies have more pressure of growth on them than the predecessors. And although there is a lot of pressure, there are still ample opportunities and unique dynamics in today's environment for business.

The strategies for entrepreneurial breakthrough are also involved in the creation of the market-buster strategies, which are basically that:

- To scrutinize the total experience of the customers and to transform it ultimately. In this strategy it is important to study the customer and the experience of the customer. It is required that the customer's consumption chain is analyzed, which is basically the series of activities that customers get engaged in, in order to meet their needs. There is a significant variation in this which depends upon the different type of product. For example, for buying a hamburger the diners or the restaurants can install take-away parcels for driving the car to the window of the diner. Similarly, in case of selling automobiles, the sellers or manufacturers can sell them online which would give the customers relief from having to come all the way to the showroom or store to buy it. The products and services can also be transformed by trying to identify the chances to either add or remove certain features, or simply by targeting more specific customers and their needs and requirements. This is also to be seen that the number of competitors in the business also has an effect on the decisive nature of the customer, and it is to be constantly inspected whether the products of the competitor is more in demand than yours.

- The second strategy focuses on the investors. The approach by which it is achieved is by redefining the metrics that drive the products by drastically modifying the significant variables which are reflected as standards of competition in an industry. The main goal of this strategy is to create advantages in the market, as well as to have a constructive effect on the stock of the firm. It is required by the entrepreneurs to analyze the 'Key metrics'. The key metrics means the amount of products or units of business that can be sold by the entrepreneur, and the total profit gained from that sale. This analysis allows the entrepreneur to redefine the main source and drive of profit.

- The third strategy is to study and scrutinize the industry and adopting a strategy to exploit the changes and shifts. There are a series of patterns of industry changes: The swings in the industry due to the cycle of scarcity and surplus; the shift in the barrier of industry that changes the power relations in the industry; the evolution of the industry naturally; and the shifts in the cost pattern that cause the chain reordering value. These shifts in the industry need to be recognized by the company in the competitive environment in order to adjust the strategy according to the shifting industries.

- The final entrepreneurial strategy is focused mainly on the emerging opportunities and adopting the ways to enter the new market. This strategy involves the innovations and invention changes that are affordable technologically, such as elevators etc.; the shift in the norms of the society which alters the behavior such as public smoking banned etc.; the change in nature or environment like global warming etc.; regulatory changes as well as institutional changes and finally the changes in demography.

The implementation of these strategies requires a meticulous analysis and a series of planning creatively done. The strategic moves for development of the entrepreneurial mindset in order for high growth are to be thoroughly followed, but it is just the beginning of the long journey that is to be taken by the aspiring entrepreneurs and managers. The success of an entrepreneur depends on the sound development of analytical techniques, constant usage of decent tools, and demonstration of a degree of discipline that we will discuss further.

The formulation of these strategies involves challenging work and thus the entrepreneurs must follow mentally through the implementation of their ideas, and take the obstacles head on while anticipating them beforehand. The process of planning requires ensuring the alignment of the desired goals and placing the work appropriately and apart from the strategies and planning. It is also required to have a creative spark in the aspirant entrepreneurs.

So in short, the corporations as well as the individuals must adopt ways of thinking regarding the business that would capture benefits from the uncertainty. This is what an entrepreneurial mindset is all about. The entrepreneurs with such a mindset go for an opportunity through planning driven by discovery, which basically involves framing, deliverables specification, testing of assumptions, reality specification of competitive market etc.

How to Build a Million-Dollar Business Using the Right Mindset

Whether an individual or an organization, the entrepreneur leaders must create a culture by developing of practices that are climate setting, where new initiatives are championed and the entrepreneurial process is orchestrated.

ABOUT THE AUTHOR

George Campbell is a successful entrepreneur and author of many business books.

George was born to a teenage mother. He and his family lived in a trailer park during his early years that's why he was exposed first-hand to poverty. However, he was a brilliant child and that brilliance earned him a scholarship to college.

Today, George is living the life he has always dreamed of for his family.

.

www.ingramcontent.com/pod-product-compliance
Lightning Source LLC
Chambersburg PA
CBHW051254170526
45165CB00004B/1710